W9-AWV-316

The Clothes We Wear

by Ellen Lawrence

Published in 2015 by Ruby Tuesday Books Ltd.

Editor: Mark J. Sachner
Designer: Emma Randall
Production: John Lingham

Photo credits:
Alamy: 7 (top left), 8, 13, 14 (right), 16–17, 22; Arctic Photos: 10–11; Cephoto, Uwe Aranas: 7 (top right), 22; Corbis: 4 (right), 22; FLPA: 5 (left); Public Domain: 7 (bottom right), 22; Shutterstock: Cover (Meunierd), 1 (Meunierd), 4 (left), 4 (center), 5 (top right: idome), 5 (bottom right: Maksim Dubinsky), 6 (left), 6 (right: Meunierd), 9 (Jacek Kadaj), 12 (left), 12 (right: Don Mammoser), 14 (left: Ninelle), 14 (center), 15 (left: wdeon), 15 (top right: Kobby Dagan), 15 (bottom right: Vicki L. Miller), 18 (Lucarelli Temistocle), 19 (left/bottom right: Kanokratnok), 19 (top right: Sandra van der Steen), 20 (left: Daniel Prudek), 20 (center: Steffen Foerster), 20 (right), 21 (top left: utcon), 21 (bottom left), 21 (right: Anton Ivanov), 22, 23; Uniesert: 7 (bottom left), 22.

Library of Congress Control Number: 2014958146

ISBN 978-1-910549-14-8

Printed and published in the United States of America

For further information including rights and permissions requests, please contact our Customer Service Department at 877-337-8577.

The picture on the front cover of this book shows Quechua children from Peru. Turn to page 8 to find out more about the colorful clothes they are wearing.

Contents

Words shown in **bold** in the text are explained in the glossary.

All the places in this book are shown on the map on page 22.

The Clothes We Wear

From T-shirts, jeans, and hats, to sweaters, coats, dresses, and scarves—every day, we all wear clothes. How do we choose which clothes to wear?

On hot days, we choose clothes that keep us cool.

On cold days, we choose clothes that keep us warm.

We choose our clothes to show what's important to us.

We choose clothes that show who we are.

We wear clothes that show what we believe.

Dressed for School

Every morning, children around the world wake up and get dressed for school. Many children put on a school uniform. Others can choose what clothes to wear for their day.

On the school bus in the United States

Off to school in the city of Nairobi in Kenya

Most kids in the United Kingdom wear a school uniform.

These girls go to school in Malaysia.

These school uniforms in Brazil show off the colors of the country's flag.

These kids are on their way to school in India.

Colorful Quechua Clothes

High in the Andes Mountains in Peru, Quechua people raise sheep, alpacas, and llamas. They use the wool from their animals to **weave** and knit colorful fabrics and clothes.

Women and girls wear skirts and jackets made from wool.

They also wear hats in many different designs.

Men and boys wear *ponchos* and hats with earflaps called *chullos*.

It's **traditional** for a father to knit a baby's first chullo.

Wool is dyed many colors. Then it is woven into cloth.

An alpaca

A chullo

A poncho

Quechua children help their parents care for the family's animals. Alpacas might look like a type of large sheep, but they're not. Alpacas and llamas are actually related to camels.

Sandals made from recycled tires

9

Clothes From Reindeer

When you live in a place that's much colder than the inside of a freezer, how do you keep warm?

Nenets people in Siberia wear clothes made from reindeer skins and fur.

The Nenets are reindeer **herders**.

They move from place to place finding food for their animals.

Nenets women sew reindeer skins together to make warm clothes and boots.

Reindeer skin boots reach right to the tops of a person's legs.

A reindeer skin coat is made from the skins of several different reindeer. It may have a hood and sleeves with built-in gloves. Some coats have the fur on the inside. Others have it on the outside.

A tent, called a *chum*, made from reindeer skins

A Nenets boy wearing a reindeer skin coat

Beautiful Saris

In India, women and girls have worn saris for more than 2,000 years. A sari is a long piece of brightly colored cloth.

A sari is draped, or wrapped, around the body to give many different looks.

The end of the sari can be draped over the head like a scarf.

These girls are wearing highly decorative saris at a festival.

Embroidery

Saris come in many different fabrics. Some saris are plain, while others are decorated with **embroidery**, beads, and even tiny mirrors. A sari can be up to 27 feet (8 m) long.

Under a sari, women and girls wear a long skirt.

They also wear a short, tight-fitting blouse called a *choli*.

These women wear saris to go to work on a farm.

Celebrating Our Roots

Sometimes we wear traditional or special clothes to celebrate a festival or holiday.

Some traditional costumes look like the clothes our **ancestors** wore.

These boys are dancing at a folk festival in Bulgaria.

These girls are at a festival on the island of Tenerife, Spain.

During the Kwanzaa festival, African Americans proudly wear clothes from their ancestors' homelands in Africa.

Every year, hundreds of Native American **powwows** are held across North America. At a powwow, Native people celebrate the traditions of their ancestors. They wear traditional clothes and perform traditional songs and dances. They also celebrate the culture of their tribes today.

Fantastic Headdresses

The Long Horn Miao people live in China. For special occasions and festivals, women and girls wear beautiful embroidered clothes. They also wear dramatic headdresses.

To create her headdress, first a girl attaches a pair of wooden horns to her head.

Then a large bundle of fabric, black wool, and real hair is placed on the horns.

The wig-like bundle is tied in place with a long, white ribbon.

Wooden horns

This girl's mother is helping her make her headdress.

The real hair in a girl's headdress is from her female ancestors. Long Horn Miao women have very long hair. That's because once a girl reaches 18, she never cuts her hair again.

Maasai Clothes

On the grasslands of Kenya and Tanzania live the Maasai people. Men, women, and children wear clothes in very bright colors—especially red.

Maasai people wear a blanket, or cloak, around their shoulders.

The cloak is called a *shuka*.

A shuka might be just one color, or it could have a striped or checked pattern.

A shuka

The color red is a sacred color to the Maasai people. This means it is very important to their beliefs. They believe that red helps keep them safe from wild animals, such as lions.

Maasai boys wearing shukas

A beaded collar

Maasai people
make and wear
lots of jewelry
made of beads.

Sandals
made from
car tires

Ankle
bracelet

All Around the World

What piece of clothing do we wear to school, at playtime, for sports, and even to bed?

It's colorful and comfortable, and kids wear it all around the world.

It's the T-shirt!

Nepal

Ecuador

Australia

Sometimes a favorite T-shirt gets too small, so you might give it to a **charity**. Then the charity can send it to another country where people need clothes. Your T-shirt might be sold in a market and soon become another kid's favorite piece of clothing!

Vietnam

Canada

Ghana

Where in the World?

Canada
Pages 4 and 21

Tenerife, Spain
Page 14

United Kingdom
Page 7

Bulgaria
Page 14

Israel
Page 5

Nepal
Page 20

Siberia, Russia
Pages 10–11

China
Pages 16–17

North
America

Europe

Asia

United States
Pages 6, 14, and 15

Africa

Vietnam
Page 21

Ecuador
Page 20

South
America

Ghana
Page 21

India
Pages 7 and 12–13

Australia

Malaysia
Pages 5 and 7

Peru
Pages 8–9

Argentina
Page 4

Brazil
Page 7

Tanzania
Pages 18–19

Kenya
Pages 5 and 6

Australia
Pages 4 and 20

22

Glossary

ancestor (AN-sess-tur)
A relative who lived a long time ago. For example, your great-grandparents and great-great-grandparents are your ancestors.

charity (CHAR-uh-tee)
An organization that raises money and uses it to do good work such as helping people living in poverty.

embroidery (em-BROI-duh-ree)
Creating a picture or pattern on a piece of cloth by making many small stitches with thread.

herder (HUR-dur)
A person who spends his or her life caring for animals and moving, or herding, them from place to place so that the animals have enough to eat.

powwow (POW-wow)
A ceremony in North America where large numbers of Native people, usually from many tribes, gather to feast, dance, sing, and honor the traditions of their ancestors.

traditional (truh-DI-shuh-nuhl)
Something that has been done in a certain way for many years by a group of people. For example, wearing certain clothes or celebrating a particular event.

weave (WEEV)
To make fabric from long pieces of wool by tightly threading, or weaving, them together.

Index

A
alpacas 8–9

B
Brazil 7, 22
Bulgaria 14, 22

C
charities 20
China 16–17, 22

E
embroidery 12, 16

F
festivals 12, 14, 16

I
India 7, 12–13, 22

K
Kenya 6, 18, 22

L
Long Horn Miao
    people 16–17

M
Maasai people 18–19

N
Nenets people 10–11

P
Peru 8–9, 22
powwows 15

Q
Quechua people 8–9

R
reindeer 10–11

S
saris 12–13

school uniforms 6–7
shoes and boots 9, 10,
    19
Siberia, Russia 10, 22

T
T-shirts 4, 20–21
Tanzania 18–19, 22

U
United Kingdom 7, 22
United States 6, 22

Read More

Adamson, Heather. *Clothes in Many Cultures (Life Around the World)*. North Mankato, MN: Capstone Press (2007).

Lewis, Clare. *Clothes Around the World (Acorn)*. North Mankato, MN: Heinemann-Raintree (2015).

Learn More Online

To learn more about clothes around the world, go to
www.rubytuesdaybooks.com/clothes